How to be
SALT AND LIGHT

The Christian's Guide to Voting

*I have known Liz Joy for nearly two decades. She is a passionate follower of Jesus Christ, passionate about the Word of God and a passionate patriot. She is fearless in standing for Truth and uprightness, and desperately desires to see the United States of America return to her Judeo-Christian roots and to live by the standards established by our founding fathers. **"How to be Salt and Light: The Christian's Guide to Voting"** is an excellent guide of sound Biblical and historical reasons as to why it is imperative for every believer to get out and vote according to the principles of the Word of God. She explains the principles with clarity and precision. Liz definitely did her homework and I highly recommend that every American read this book and then do it!*

Sandy Ross, Women's Pastor, Summit Christian Center, Founder of Women of Excellence Ministries, San Antonio, Texas

With a passion to ignite and engage the voter to become active in the political process, Liz Joy, has put together a guide for voting that will help clarify the biblical perspective of how to vote. Liz's call is for all to sew a seed with their right to vote and do it with God's guidelines in place. I applaud Liz for encouraging and urging us to be engaged in a process that we are so blessed to be able to be a part of. It is so important in today's culture and society that the voter has this information, so they will be able to make an informed decision based on biblical principles.

New York State Senator George Amedore Jr., President Amedore Group, Albany, New York

I encourage the reader to be positively inspired by this book. Liz Joy is a lady of great integrity, love and conviction. She has a passion to help believers and society as a whole, to make decisions which promote Christ, liberty and wholeness to our nation. God bless you Liz as you fulfill God's calling for your life.

Dr. Mark F Jones, Licensed Marriage & Family Therapist, Founder & Owner of Liberty Alliance Group, San Antonio, Texas

More than ever, we desperately need Christians to care for their communities, state and nation. Prayer and exercising the privilege of voting are two responsibilities we must not neglect. We can choose leaders with a Biblical worldview and Liz helps readers to understand this critical need and how to get started.
Cindy Asmussen, Legislative Director, Ethics & Religious Liberty Advisor, Austin, Texas

Liz has a passion for America. In these times of political division, confusion, and misinformation, where does one go to find the truth so they can know how to vote? Of course, the answer is where all truth is found, The Bible. Liz has done us all a favor. She has searched the Word of God, and been led by the Holy Spirit. God has given us a clear guide in making decisions that reflect His will when we vote in an election. I highly encourage everyone to read this book and apply these principles every time they vote.
Keith Legg, Pastor of Full Gospel Tabernacle, Gansevoort, NY and House 2 House, a Home Church in Scotia, NY

How to be

SALT AND LIGHT

THE CHRISTIAN'S GUIDE TO VOTING

By Liz Lemery Joy

Life Bridge Press

HOW TO BE SALT AND LIGHT: THE CHRISTIAN'S GUIDE TO VOTING
© 2016 by Liz Lemery Joy

These books are available at special discounts when purchased in quantity for use as premiums, promotions, fundraising, and educational use. For inquiries and details, contact: info@suedetweiler.com. Published by Life Bridge Press, a division of Detweiler LLC.

ISBN TPB: 978-1-943613-80-9

ISBN eBook: 978-1-943613-81-6

Cover Design by Britt Dodson

Editing and Production by Life Bridge Press, a division of Detweiler LLC.

Scripture quotations marked (NLT) are taken from the Holy Bible, New Living Translation.

Copyright© 1996, 2004, 2007, 2013 by Tyndale House Foundation. Used by permission of Tyndale House Publishers, Inc., Carol Stream, Illinois 60188. All rights reserved.

Scripture taken from the New King James Version®. Copyright © 1982 by Thomas Nelson. Used by permission. All rights reserved.

Scripture quotations marked (NIV) are taken from the Holy Bible, New International Version®, NIV®. Copyright © 1973, 1978, 1984, 2011 by Biblica, Inc.™ Used by permission of Zondervan. All rights reserved worldwide. www.zondervan.com. The "NIV" and "New International Version" are trademarks registered in the United States Patent and Trademark Office by Biblica, Inc.™

Scriptures marked AMP are taken from the AMPLIFIED BIBLE (AMP): Scripture taken from the AMPLIFIED® BIBLE, Copyright © 1954, 1958, 1962, 1964, 1965, 1987 by the Lockman Foundation. Used by Permission.

Scripture quotations taken from the Amplified® Bible (AMPC), Copyright © 1954, 1958, 1962, 1964, 1965, 1987 by The Lockman Foundation.

Used by permission. www.Lockman.org.

Scripture quotations marked "MSG" or "The Message" are taken from The Message. Copyright 1993, 1994, 1995, 1996, 2000, 2001, 2002. Used by permission of NavPress Publishing Group.

DEDICATION

I dedicate this book to my own children and future grand-children.

Nathan, Katharine, Luke and Brooke, you are all fearfully and wonderfully made. I'm so glad God picked me to be your Mom. I love you all dearly.

I also dedicate this book to every Christian voter in America, both present and future. I pray you always choose life and blessing, so that you and your descendants will live and that through biblical voting, you leave a good inheritance, to your children and grand-children.

FORWARD

The importance of this book cannot be overstated. It is imperative that we as believers understand this one fundamental truth, voting for us is not a right, but a responsibility. Once that is understood the truths set forth in this book will remove the "guesswork" that so many Christians deal with concerning voting.

Liz does a masterful job of laying out a biblical case explaining the believer's responsibility, but also follows it up with practical evidence of what the Bible says we must consider when we vote. We have to understand "who" we represent when casting our ballot & what's important to Him.

In my opinion, this book should be required reading in every church and its truths spoken from every pulpit in America. Once you read this I encourage you to do two things: Do what it says and share it with others!

Tim Fox
Political Analyst/ Co-Host
America Stands-Election Coverage in the Spirit of Faith
Americastands.us
Fort Worth, Texas

SECTION ONE

CALLED TO BE SALT AND LIGHT

"You are the salt of the earth; but if the salt loses its flavor, how shall it be seasoned? It is then good for nothing but to be thrown out and trampled underfoot by men." Matthew 5:13 (NKJV)

Did you catch that? You are salt. As a follower of Christ, you are the seasoning God uses to bring out the goodness within all of His creation. Without you, there is nothing to bring out the nourishing elements He embedded in this world.

It's important to notice there are two parts to Matthew 5:13. First, Jesus tells us what we are, and then, with the next breath he warns us of what will happen if we lose our purpose— we will be thrown out, and trampled under the feet of men.

You won't get very far into a daily news cycle before you see the evidence of this truth being played out before your eyes. Our Christian faith and brothers and sisters in Christ are being trampled under the feet of a perverse culture weighted with an onslaught of ungodly laws.

It's easy to feel as if the days are growing darker with each passing election. That, there is nothing you can do. You might tell yourself that it's just happening the way the bible said it would. Maybe you believe that your faith is personal, and shouldn't be tainted with the nastiness of politics. The old adage of voting for the "lesser of two evils" doesn't sit well. When these are our prevailing thoughts, it's tempting to believe the right thing to do is to not vote at all.

As Christians, relinquishing our vote is not an option.

We have only two choices: be the salt and the light Jesus called us to be, or continue to be thrown out and trampled upon.

Salt and light change everything it touches. The deepest blackness cannot blot out the light, it enhances it. Salt makes you want to savor the goodness. It preserves that which would have rotted without it. That's how Jesus called us to impact our culture.

You can answer this call by representing the Kingdom of God in all elections. It is a profound responsibility we have as the Body of Jesus Christ, to be fervently involved in steering this country toward the righteousness of God.

This guide is for the Christian who wants to be salt and light to a dying world. You can learn how to follow God's heart amid the rhetoric of men. You don't have to be a biblical scholar or political activist. As a matter of fact, God makes it very simple.

Ambassadors for Jesus Christ

"So we are ambassadors for Christ, as though God were making His appeal through us; we, as Christ's representatives." 2 Corinthians 5:20 (AMP)

Ambassadors of Jesus Christ, that is who we are. So what does an ambassador do? What is the role and obligation of an ambassador?

The definition of ambassador: A diplomatic official of the highest rank, sent by one sovereign or state, or government to represent it. A diplomatic official serving as permanent head of a country's mission.

An authorized messenger, an authorized representative, a diplomatic official of the Kingdom of Heaven. We are authorized representatives. We have an obligation to represent Heaven's mission in all things. We are sons and daughters of the Most-High, the King of Kings.

God commanded all of us, His children, men and women alike, to be ambassadors for Jesus Christ here in this world. As ambassadors for Christ, God makes His appeal through us. He is calling and summoning us, through the word of God and by the Holy Spirit.

He expects us to answer.

Each vote we cast is a seed sown into the prosperity and direction of this nation. When we vote, we are being faithful to God's appeal. Each vote we evade is to personally ignore and neglect that request.

"Don't be misled: No one makes a fool of God. What a person plants, he will harvest."
Galatians 6:7-8 (MSG)

What we plant, what we sow, is exactly the harvest we will reap. The opposite is true. What we fail to plant, we will not be allowed to harvest.

Out of approximately 60 million Christians, roughly 30 million routinely ignore the election booth. Being apathetic about voting has allowed our country to reap a harvest of thorns. This is not the vision our founders had for America. The vision they had was one of Godly men and women serving the citizens.

"Blessed, happy, fortunate, to be envied is the nation whose God is the Lord, the people He has chosen as His heritage." Psalm 33:12 (AMP)

America was once the envy of nations.

"When the uncompromisingly righteous are in authority, the people rejoice, but when the wicked man rules the people groan and sigh." Proverbs 29:2 (AMP)

We have a whole lot of groaning and sighing going on in this nation. And yet, election after election, Christians have not risen to put Godly men and women into the majority of political offices. If 30 million Christians are sitting home on voting day, or for that matter, aren't even registered to vote how will this ever change?

We are to be bold ambassadors, specifically through our votes. We are to be actively involved in steering this nation. One of the ways we do can do that is by voting the Bible in all elections.

What does it mean to 'vote the Bible?' It means to vote the Bible's stance, the Bible's position on all political and legislative issues.

As Christians, we're to do this in all national, state, and local elections. A Christian should never miss an opportunity to vote.

How is voting a command of the Bible?

We The People

When God called his children into the promised land He instructed Moses to send twelve spies in to study the ways of the inhabitants and come back with a report. He wanted an assessment of the land, people, towns, homes, food and other ways of life. Two of the men came back with an encouraging, courageous, faithful report. But, the other ten men were terrified of what they saw. They described the people of the land as being fierce, with fortified walls and unparalleled strength.

Those ten men of God saw themselves as defeated weaklings. They complained and objected to having to fight for the land. Even though God was on their side and had already told Moses that he was giving them the land. They just couldn't get over the fear and intimidation they felt. As a result of their own apathy, and lack of faith, they never got to live in the inheritance God wanted them to have. Their refusal to participate in the process of taking the land left them with nothing…No inheritance.

Here again, we see God gives the promise, but it comes attached to an expectation of action. The Israelites were given the land, but they were still responsible for taking it. The Lord always gives the corresponding action to his people.

Jesus Christ is the same yesterday, today and forever. (Hebrews 13:8 NIV) He still works the same way today. We are responsible for the land we live in, and we too must have the corresponding action.

At another point in history, before the ink was dry, at the close of the Constitutional Convention in 1787, historians note that Dr. Benjamin Franklin was asked by a Mrs. Powell,

"Well, Doctor what have we got, a republic or a monarchy?"
Franklin replied, **"A republic...if you can keep it."**

Our republic has been slipping away over the last century. In order for you to understand why it is important to vote, you have to know what you are a part of—what the Founding Fathers have entrusted to us for safekeeping.

If you ask most people, they believe the United States is a democracy. Yet, democracy is never mentioned in the U.S. Constitution. For over a century, after our founding, it was common knowledge that America was a representative republic. There is a big difference between a republic and a democracy. Here is an easy way to remember it:

A republic is when the people *vote* to put elected officials in office. Those elected officials then make laws and the republic is governed by those laws. The elected officials, as well as the people, are bound to obey the laws.

A democracy is when the majority and sentiment of the people rule. True democracy is ruled by the people's feelings at that particular point in time. If an issue needs to be ruled upon, a vote is taken- the majority rules the decision of the outcome, *not* the law.

Do you see the difference? Democracies are based on popular feelings at the time and can vote on any issue and the majority wins. For example, if the feeling of the people is all personal property should be shared equally instead of individual ownership, then the sentiment of that majority wins and now rules the land. Property, therefore, is no longer the right of an individual to be privately owned.

Any subject or problem you can think of gets solved by majority sentiment and opinion, not the rule of law.

In a republic, laws are already set in place. These laws don't change, therefore if the right to own property is a law, then no popular vote of the people can change that just because they feel like it.

David Barton, of WallBuilders, gives an excellent definition of various governments in a 2001 article titled: Republic v. Democracy. In the article he writes:

"A republic is the highest form of government devised by man, but it also requires the greatest amount of human care and maintenance. If neglected, it can deteriorate into a variety of lesser forms, including a democracy (government conducted by popular feeling); anarchy (a system in which each person determines his own rules and standards); oligarchy (a government run by a small council or group of elite individuals); or a dictatorship (a government run by a single individual).

"As John Adams explained:
"Democracy will soon degenerate into an anarchy; such an anarchy that every man will do what is right in his own eyes and no man's life or property or reputation or liberty will be secure, and every one of these will soon [mold] itself into a system of

subordination of all the moral virtues and intellectual abilities, all the powers of wealth, beauty, wit and science, to the wanton pleasures, the capricious will, and the execrable (abominable) cruelty of one or a very few.'"

Doesn't this sound like the direction America is going in? Every man doing what's right in their own eyes? Anarchy- we've had countless attacks on police officers throughout our cities. Moral virtues on the decline? Families can hardly watch TV together anymore without their eyes and ears being assaulted by pornographic pictures and crude language. Oligarchy? A government that seems as if a small council has absorbed the power and are ruling as an elite group?

You see? There is a reason the Founding Fathers chose a republic instead of a democracy. They didn't trust a democracy and for good reason.

In The Federalist 10, [2]James Madison wrote:
"Hence it is that such democracies have ever been spectacles of turbulence and contention; have ever been found incompatible with personal security or the rights of property, and have in general been as short in their lives as they have been violent in their deaths. Theoretic politicians, who have patronized this species of government, have erroneously supposed that by reducing mankind to a perfect equality in their political rights, they would, at the same time, be perfectly equalized and assimilated in their possessions, their opinions, and their passions."

We see this taking place across the nation. Special

interest groups like Planned Parenthood take our tax money. Political Correctness dictates opinions and limits free speech. The passion of environmental movement dictates laws that impact entire communities.

In fact, our Founding Fathers considered a pure democracy akin to mob rule. Imagine you are a sheep in the company of five wolves. Now, it's time to vote on what the group will have for lunch. We have become a nation of sheep that have not followed our Shepherd's commands.

If Christians continue to fail to heed the call, we will continue to follow our ungodly leaders down the path our founders feared.

So how will we correct the course this nation is on and put our republic back on track? With these three simple steps.

Step One
Pray

"Pray especially for rulers and their governments to rule well so we can be quietly about our business of living simply, in humble contemplation. This is the way our Savior God wants us to live." 1 Timothy 2:12 (MSG)

As a Christian, you are called to be obedient and pray. We are commanded to pray for our leaders. Like them or not. Whether or not they are from your preferred party. It doesn't matter. We are commanded to pray for our rulers and government.

We are called to pray the Bible's promises over the leadership of our nation, our state, our cities, and towns so that we may live in a land of peace. On a more personal level, it means that we must pray for our leaders so we are able to live out our faith day to day. We must honor God, humble ourselves, regardless of our feelings and pray.

The Bible promises a great reward for this kind of obedience.

It promises in 2 Chronicles, that if we will humble ourselves, seek God's face, turn from wickedness and pray, that God will forgive our sins. Furthermore, he promises to restore and heal our land. That is a wonderful promise! 2 Chronicles 7:14 (NLT)

Notice, that God said "MY" people. Those who are called by His name. Is that you? Are you a follower of Christ? Then it's you and I He is referring to. We must seek God's face. Turn from our wicked ways — and pray.

Pray for our country. Pray for our leaders. The pornographers are not going to do it. The sex traffickers, the drug dealers, and the terrorists do not have to turn from their wicked ways before God will heal our land. He's talking to those of us, who seek forgiveness of our sins and seek His face. It's our responsibility, he said it to the ones he calls his.

God *wants* to heal our land.

He's left it up to us to do our part.

Step Two
Register to Vote

He who is careless in his work, is a brother to him who destroys. Proverbs 18:9 (AMP)

The obvious first step is to register to vote. I have provided a link to register[1] in the footnotes. It takes less than 5 minutes. If you are not registered, honor God, and sign up. Today is a great day to become earnestly engaged in steering this nation. There are specific dates you must register by before an election. So make sure you check your state's deadlines. I have also provided a link[2] for you to easily check your state.

Many Christians complain about the current conditions we are facing in this country. But, the truth is, if you are not voting, you have absolutely no right to complain. I will go as far as saying, if you don't vote, then by default you have sowed into the problems this nation is having to withstand. Not voting is choosing to make your God given voice (your vote) of no effect.

You can easily exchange the word "work" for "vote" in the verse above. He who is careless in his vote is a brother to him who destroys.

---

1   registertovote.org
2   "https://www.usvotefoundation.org/vote/state-elections/state-election-dates-deadlines.htm6" https://www.usvotefoundation.org/vote/state-elections/state-election-dates-deadlines.htm6

So many times I've heard one person or another say they didn't have time to vote or the weather was bad, their favorite show was on and they didn't want to miss it. I've also heard it was bath night for the kids or they had too much homework. While I realize getting in the car and driving to the polling center may be inconvenient, think of the repercussions of not voting.

God instructs us in Proverbs 22 to train up our children in the way they should go, and when they are older they will not stray from it. After all, we are told to teach our children how to pray. We teach them to go to church, love God and read their Bible. Shouldn't we also teach them how to vote? I encourage you to bring them with you into the booth and let them see the process in action. You are allowed to do that. I always brought my kids with me and let them see me cast my votes. Somehow, I managed to cram five of us behind the curtain. You can too. Children learn by what we model for them.

As Christians, we are called to be good stewards of that which God has entrusted to us. Use your vote to work for the well-being of this nation.

Step Three
Vote Biblically

As ambassadors of Jesus Christ, we need to know how to vote Biblically. A Christian's mission is to stand firm on the Bible's stance on all political and legislative issues we face as a nation.

Therefore, we need to be familiar, confident and able to represent the Bible's mandates in the voting booth.

How do we know what the most important issues are? How do we choose what to put first? There's so much to think about. It can be very confusing. Some of the most concerning matters in the United States are:

Economy
National debt
Terrorism
National security
Immigration
Abortion described as Women's Reproductive Rights
Taxation
Global warming
Healthcare
The refugee crisis
Feeding the poor
Energy
Marriage laws
Racial tensions

The news media, talk shows, and political candidates are all saying what they think the top priorities are. Our ears are bombarded daily with differing opinions. But, we need to ask ourselves, what does God say? In order to be effective ambassadors of Jesus Christ, we need to know.

The good news is that God is very clear in His word.

Not on My Watch: Preserving Freedom Through Biblical Voting
"A good man leaves an inheritance to his children's children..."
Proverbs 13:22 (NKJV)

In 1967 at the dawn of President Reagan's political career, the newly elected Governor Ronald Reagan gave one of his most compelling speeches as his inaugural address. He spoke of how the change of power is so seamlessly done here in the United States. So much so, that we consider it commonplace. And yet, it is a near miracle to many of the world's inhabitants. He went on to say what a marvel it is to peacefully delegate this power and yet retain custody of it.

"Perhaps you and I have lived with this miracle too long to be properly appreciative. Freedom is a fragile thing and is never more than one generation away from extinction. It is not ours by inheritance; it must be fought for and defended constantly by each generation, for it comes only once to a people. Those who have known freedom and then lost it have never known it again..."

Reagan went on to quote and agree with 18th Century philosopher Montesquieu,

"The deterioration of every government begins with the decay of the principle upon which it was founded.' This is true today as it was when it was written in 1748.[1]"

From Christopher Columbus, who believed God had chosen him and charted the course using his Bible, to the early puritans who sought to live righteously before God without persecution, to the Founding Fathers America was envisioned as being a "city on a hill" an example of righteous living to the world.

We have inherited our country, but it is ours to keep or lose with each generation. This is the hour that we, as Christians, must stand up and be counted in order for God's will to prevail for His people. We must know the heart of God, so we can be effective ambassadors for Christ and salt and light to a lost world.

God didn't call all of us to be political scholars, but he did call all of us to be faithful with what He has given us. He clearly lays out His priorities for us and our nation.

---

[1] "https://www.reaganlibrary.archives.gov/archives/speeches/gov-speech/01051967a.htm"

The Author of Life

"If you really love Me, you will keep and obey My commandments." John 14:15 (AMP)

As Christians, we must change our views and opinions to line up with God's word. Honoring God means obeying His word. Obeying His commands is how we show Him love.

In the first five books of the old testament, there are roughly 613 laws. However, God took these 613 laws and centered in on the ten most important. They're known as the Ten Commandments.

Guess which issue made God's top ten? It also happens to be one of the top issues of major contention in every political race. Abortion. Abortion is not a war on women like many people claim. Nor is abortion a reproductive right. No, abortion is a war on the womb and the Bible proves it.

God himself created the womb when he fashioned woman in the Garden of Eden. The life within a woman's womb is supposed to be the safest, most pleasant place in the entire world for a developing baby.

In defiance, America itself has made it a war zone that has killed 58,586,256 babies since the passing of Roe Vs. Wade in 1973. Without a doubt, God had unique and special plans for each one of these precious lives. Psalm 139 confirms God's well thought out intentions and purpose, in advance, for every single developing baby boy and girl:

You made all the delicate, inner parts of my body and knit me together in my mother's womb.

Thank you for making me so wonderfully complex! Your workmanship is marvelous—how well I know it.

You watched me as I was being formed in utter seclusion, as I was woven together in the dark of the womb.

You saw me before I was born. Every day of my life was recorded in your book. Every moment was laid out before a single day had passed. Psalm 139: 13-16 (NLT)

Here are the recorded death tolls of U.S. soldiers in all the wars America has fought:
[1]

War of Independence: 8,000
War of 1812: 2,260
Civil War: 620,000
World War 1: 118,000
World War 2: 405,000
Korean War: 54,000
Vietnam: 58,000
Gulf War: 294
Afghanistan: 2,229

TOTAL: 1,267,783

1 "https://www.quora.com/How-does-history-compare-abortion-victims-to-war-casualties-in-the-United-States" https://www.quora.com/How-does-history-compare-abortion-victims-to-war-casualties-in-the-United-States "https://en.wikipedia.org/wiki/Women%2527s_Equality_Party_(New_York)?oldformat=true" https://en.wikipedia.org/wiki/Women%27s_Equality_Party_(New_York)?oldformat=true

1,267,783 soldiers have lost their precious lives fighting in war since the year 1775. Compare that to 58,586,256 innocent babies who have lost their lives in abortion since 1973 alone. There have been 57,318,473 more babies killed by abortion than all of the recorded casualties of American soldiers in all wars since 1775. These numbers are nothing short of horrific.

One of the Ten Commandments, God's top commands to His children is: "You shall not murder."

Murder is the act of killing a human being with premeditation or planning. Make no mistake, abortion is killing a human being on purpose and with planning.

I want to gently pause for a moment and explain, that if you have had an abortion, or you encouraged or facilitated someone into having an abortion, there is absolute forgiveness for you.

God will forgive you for that right here, right now. Just bring your burden to Jesus, confess it to him, ask for forgiveness and receive his abundant, merciful, kind, gracious, loving, forgiveness and restoration.

The Bible promises us that Jesus paid the price for us, and 1John1:9 says that "The Lord won't let us down; he'll be true to himself. He'll forgive our sins and purge us of all wrongdoing." The Lord will never fail to forgive you. Never. I want to reassure you of that.

So, in explaining about abortion, please hear me, I'm not condemning you. God loves you, and He's ready to forgive with open arms. I encourage you to receive and embrace that forgiveness. Today is a new day. His faithful love never runs out, and His mercies are new every morning. So take heart, and keep reading.

The faithful love of the Lord never ends! His mercies never cease. Great is his faithfulness; his mercies begin afresh each morning.
Lamentations 3:22 (NLT)

Therefore, the Bible is clear that protecting innocent life is God's most important issue when examining the candidates running for political office.

Subsequently, the very first thing we must look at and examine when comparing candidates, is determining where that candidate stands on the issue of life.

Again, if you are a Christian, and you want to vote Biblically, you must never choose a candidate that supports abortion. Why? You ask. Because God honors life first. He's the creator of life. He's a God of order, and we can't take the things we think are most important and rearrange God's order. (1Corinthians 14)

We can't vote with our feelings, or vote what's best for our wallets. No, we vote Heaven's stance, regardless of what political party we are registered with, or what our parents, grandparents or worker's union has always done.

This is so important. When a Christian walks into the voting booth, we are not there to represent the Republican party, the Democratic party, the Independent, Green or new Women's Equality party[1] (established in New York State 2014).

1   Note:[1] If you live in New York, don't be deceived by that title. The Women's Equality Party supports third-trimester abortion up until the time of birth.

As Christians, we represent the Lord. We're *His* ambassadors. Our loyalty is not to a political party and just voting across a specific party line. Too many Christians get deceived in politics. They focus in on issues they've contrived in their own mindsets to be most important. The biggest deception Christians are falling into is simply not remembering that as is Christ, so are we in this world. (1John 4:17)

This simply means we say, act and do exactly what the Word says. This includes the voting booth and coming into alignment with what the Bible says about protecting innocent life.

In John 12:49 Jesus said he doesn't speak of himself, but of the Father that sent him. It is the same with us. We don't speak for ourselves in the voting booth. We don't leave Jesus outside the booth, tell him we'll be right back, then go in and vote however we feel like it. No, we faithfully answer God's appeal and speak (vote) of the Father. We are His.

I'm telling you, voting this way is going to get you blessed! When you vote for life, you are planting good seed, and you will reap a good harvest.

In talking about political parties, I want to point out that all political parties have public written platforms, which spell out exactly what they stand for. When you sign up and register for a political party you need to know that you are putting your written name on that party's platform. Meaning, you are actually coming into agreement and becoming officially affiliated with that party. I have put a link at the back of this book for you to read the platforms.

For this reason, if that party is pro-abortion, otherwise described as pro-choice, I would highly suggest you refuse to link your name to that party line. If you are already registered and the political party you are part of is pro-abortion or pro-choice, I would propose you remove your name and choose a pro-life party, one that will protect innocent life.

We should always do our best as Christians not to be aligned with people whose written manifesto includes shedding innocent blood. The Bible is very clear in Proverbs that the Lord Himself hates hands that shed innocent blood. If you knowingly assign your own name to a political party advocating abortion and choice, you are indeed joining with those who support shedding innocent blood.

You are also taking part in sowing the seeds of abortion. Therefore, the harvest you reap will be aligned with murder. That may sound harsh, but it's the truth.

Again, let me reiterate, if that's you, simply repent, embrace forgiveness and make a change. Today is a new day and a God-given opportunity to humbly make an adjustment.

Remember, the purpose of this book is to help God's children be salt and light by actively steering this country. No one can expect to reap blessing and prosperity if they're sowing to murder. God wants you and America on a blessed and prosperous path.

Deuteronomy 30:19 says: "Today I have given you the choice between life and death, between blessings and curses. Now, I call on heaven and earth to witness the choice you make."

And just in case Christians aren't sure what choice to make, between life or death, God is so kind, so good, and merciful, that He even gives us the answer. He goes on to say...

"Oh, that you would choose life, so that you and your descendants might live!"

We can substitute the word vote in that verse. You see when you vote, you're choosing and when you're choosing, you're voting.

So let's read it again. "Today, I have given you the vote between life and death, between blessings and curses. Now, I call on heaven and earth to witness the vote you make."

"Oh, that you would VOTE life, so that you and your descendants might live!"

Make no mistake, God is personally watching our votes. Heaven is watching how we vote. *"I call on heaven and earth to witness the choice (the vote) you make"*

That's powerful!

How can we expect to have descendants in the land of the free and the home of the brave if we have killed them at a rate of almost 60 million souls since

1973? 60 million Americans that could have been. They represent lives that may have been business owners, teachers, doctors, Nobel prize winners, soldiers, scientists, firefighters, police officers, lawyers, builders, Olympians, fathers, mothers, brothers, sisters. Let that sink in. What have we allowed on our watch? Is it any wonder our republic is suffering and groaning? Is it any wonder we have such economic instability when we have annihilated 60 million fellow Americans?

I believe that millions of people in this nation are not prospering in their spirits, souls and bodies, because of the votes they are sowing, the seeds they're sowing, and they may not even realize it. God's word clearly states,

"My people are destroyed for lack of knowledge."
Hosea 4:6

For example, New York State has the highest abortion rate in the country, so much so that in 2012 alone, more black babies were killed in abortion in New York, than were actually even born. That's tragic!

In direct correlation to the abortions, New York State is sowing, it is also one of the least prosperous States in the country. It is rated last among all 50 states for economic [1]freedom. It has some of the highest taxes and business regulations. Even with all that tax money, New York State still isn't prospering. Sadly, it never will, until New York Christians actively put men and women in

---

1   "https://www.fraserinstitute.org/studies/economic-free-dom-of-north-america-2015-annual-report" https://www.fraserinstitute.org/studies/economic-freedom-of-north-america-2015-annual-report

office, who will pass legislation protecting and preserving innocent life.

In November of 2015, the Center for Disease Control released its' national abortion report on the number of babies who die every year here in the United States. 58,250 die in abortion every month; 13,442 die in abortion every week, and 1,915 die every single day. 699,000 babies every year are killed in abortion, right here on American soil. Our ears have become deaf to their cries.

Of those 699,000 – One-half of one percent are due to rape or the mother's health being at risk, meaning 99.5% of these abortions are simply by choice or by vote.

Perhaps you're reading these statistics and you think that abortion shouldn't be a legislative issue, you don't think it has any room in the political arena and that it should be a personal choice.

The truth is government leaders are the ones legislating it. They are mandating government funds and taxpayer money to pay for it. They are also writing and passing laws demanding corporations include abortion in their medical coverage to employees. It's the legislators themselves that have made this a political issue. They run on political tickets declaring reproductive rights for women to choose to do whatever they want with a pregnancy right up until the time of birth.

Yet, science itself has proven that at 20 weeks' gestation a baby in the womb recognizes its mother's voice, can hiccup, suck its thumb, swallow, kick and feel immense pain. Therefore, as Christians, ambassadors for Jesus Christ who represent Heaven's stance, we must respond with the Bible's answer on this issue in the voting booth.

You now know that protecting innocent life is first and foremost in choosing a candidate. Notably, that means every candidate, from the school board, mayor, county legislature, sheriff, judges, assemblymen and women, senators, governors all the way up to the White House.

Maybe you question why you must choose pro-life candidates in every circumstance, for every office, including seemingly small leadership positions? Because, how a candidate values life determines where they'll put a value on all other things and everything else they'll do in office. The decisions they make, based on the moral compass they have, has a direct ripple effect on the prosperity of the community you live in. God is the creator of life. He honors life. When we honor Him, He promises to honor us.
(1Samuel 2:30)

Understandably, because people are human, there are no perfect candidates out there. So, we are to vote as close to the Bible as we can get. Matthew 6:33 says: Seek first His kingdom and His righteousness, His way of doing things and all these things will be given to you as well.

Just keeping these first things first, you're going to get blessed. Honestly, for the last 10 years of United States elections, if you can just answer the life issue between candidates, then you'll know exactly how to vote. These days, candidates are very vocal about where they stand so, you'll usually immediately have your answer.

Interestingly, you may have your answer on the life issue, but not like anything else that candidate stands for. Don't compromise, put life first and God will honor your obedience to Him.

I have repeatedly heard Christians say that because they don't like the choices or personalities of the candidates they aren't going to vote. This is not the right answer and again the Bible proves it. Your vote is your seed. So if you choose not to vote, you have chosen to be silent on behalf of heaven. You have chosen to disobey the Bible's command to be an ambassador for Jesus Christ.

You are honoring God with your vote. It's an act of obedience to Him. If you don't like the candidates, their stances, their personalities or their rhetoric, it may be helpful to remind yourself that you are not personally honoring the candidate with your vote. The vote is between you and God. It's for him! The Lord will reward your obedience. You can have complete peace knowing you were faithful, loyal and acted as a good steward by voicing Heaven's stance and the Father's mandate in the voting booth. Remove the candidates' personalities and rhetoric out of your thoughts. Instead, fix your eyes on the Lord- Him and Him alone.

Israel

"Anyone who hits you, hits me-bloodies my nose, blackens my eye..." Zechariah 2: 8-9 (MSG)

The next thing we must look at after the life issue when choosing a candidate is their stance on Israel. Are they looking to divide and compromise Israel? Or will they support, protect and defend Israel?

How a nation treats Israel is very important and cannot be overlooked. God blesses the nations that bless Israel, and there is judgment for those nations that curse Israel.

Again, the Bible is very clear and proves God's stance on Israel.

"And I will make you a great nation, And I will bless you abundantly, And make your name great, exalted, distinguished; And you shall be a blessing, a source of great good to others; And I will bless, do good for, benefit, those who bless you, And I will curse, that is, subject to My wrath and judgment, the one who curses despises, dishonors, has contempt for you. And in you all the families (nations) of the earth will be blessed." Genesis 12: 2-3 (AMP)

Furthermore, Zechariah 2:8 explains that whoever touches Israel, bloodies God's nose and blackens his eye. Personally, I would never want to be in a position where I have done that to the Lord! Another version says that whoever touches Israel, touches the apple of God's eye. (King James Version) Certainly, God does not mince words when speaking about Israel.

We know that the Word of God promises us that the Lord never changes. So, His views on Israel haven't changed either.

Malachi 3:6 says, "I am the Lord and I change not."

Hebrews 13:8 says, "Jesus Christ is the same yesterday, today and forever."

Therefore, as ambassadors of Christ, our stance on Israel must be the same as the Lord's: one of total support, defense, protection, and prayer.

Pray for the peace of Jerusalem:
"May they prosper who love you, holy city.

"May peace be within your walls And prosperity within your palaces."

For the sake of my brothers and my friends, I will now say, "May peace be within you."

For the sake of the house of the Lord our God, which is Jerusalem, I will seek your (the city's) good. Psalm 122: 6-9 (AMP)

Let me reiterate: Examine the candidates, seek to protect innocent life first, then look for the one that will stand with, support, and protect Israel!

It will be very rare that you'll have two candidates, in opposing political parties, running against each other, that both agree on protecting innocent life, and protecting Israel.

The Sanctity of Biblical Marriage

After you have established which candidate will 1) Protect innocent life and 2) Support Israel, then you need to move on to the final issue and that is marriage. Marriage is an established covenant between man, woman, and God. Marriage was created by God Himself.

For this reason, a man shall leave his father and his mother, and shall be joined to his wife; and they shall become one flesh. And the man and his wife were both naked and were not ashamed or embarrassed. Genesis 2: 24-25 (AMP)

Mark 10: 7-9 confirms again that, in marriage, a husband and wife are no longer two, but one flesh. Their parts are created by God, and they fit together perfectly... one flesh...Therefore, what God has joined together, let no one separate.

"For this reason a man shall leave his father and his mother, to establish a home with his wife, and the two shall become one flesh; so that they are no longer two, but are united as one flesh. Therefore, what God has united and joined together, man must not separate by divorce."
Mark 10:7-9 (AMP)

There is an epidemic going on right now in this nation and around the world. It's happening in Godly,

Christian families and it's the issue of lesbian, gay, bisexual, transgender and queer confusion. To say that this is a worldly problem only isn't true. This is happening at sweeping proportions in Christian families.

As the body of Christ, we need to help families stand strong, in love, on what the Bible says. The devil has launched an all-out attack on marriage and families. The problem itself isn't lesbianism, gay, bisexual, transgender and queer confusion (LGBTQ). This is just a symptom of the real issue. The root of all of this is Satan's weapon, planned and forged specifically to cause confusion and doubt in someone's true identity in Jesus Christ.

It's all about Satan trying to steal, kill and destroy someone's true, God-given identity, by causing that person to doubt, question, and wonder who they really are.

Truthfully, this tactic isn't anything new. Satan started this kind of trickery in the Garden of Eden when he tempted Eve with thoughts of who she really was. In Genesis Chapter Three, Satan made statements to Eve that weren't true. He insinuated God was withholding from her, by instructing her not to eat of the tree of the knowledge of good and evil.

The Devil told her that if she ate the fruit forbidden by God, her eyes would be opened and she'd be just like God. In other words, he started with doubt…*Did God really say you shouldn't eat from that tree, Eve? Well, God only told you that because he knows if you did eat, you'd finally have your eyes opened…you'll finally be just like God… (Paraphrase- mine).*

Seemingly, he tried to convince her that she wasn't

like God already. He tried to get her to think God was withholding from her. *If you eat this fruit, you'll have more freedom... you'll see things better... You'll be more content. If you just abandon what God said, you'll have something better... (Paraphrase-mine).*

Nothing could have been further from the truth. Eve got Adam to eat the fruit too, and by that evening both of them were afraid, ashamed and hiding from God. Going against God's ways never brings a blessing. Thankfully, the Lord is always good. He forgave both of them and made provision.

Just like Adam and Eve, nobody starts out purposely trying to be tricked and deceived. So, as the body of Christ, we must help each other and lovingly share truth when someone is deceived with lesbian, gay, bi-sexual, transgender and queer (LGBTQ) confusion. We must recognize their struggle.

Satan's plan is to bombard someone's mind with thought, after thought, after thought, until he makes an in-road. Those thoughts turn into questions: *Am I really who God says I am? Was I really made to be a boy? Was I really made to be a girl? Do I really like the opposite sex? I think I prefer the same sex. Maybe I'm not who I thought I was? I think I'm in the wrong body. I feel trapped.*

If someone is regularly perplexed about their true identity, then they eventually speak words according to that uncertainty. Words become actions and after actions comes a changed belief system. At that point, the person begins to declare they are of the LGBTQ community and tries to walk in a new and different identity from the one they were destined and designed by God to be born into.

It is so important for the body of Christ to respond in love, kindness, and mercy to all those who are struggling within the church, or within their own families, with the battle of same-sex desires thoughts, actions, and behaviors. It is grossly inappropriate and cruel for any Christian to ever respond cold-heartedly or with callous jokes. This kind of behavior mocks someone God very lovingly and thoughtfully created.

Christians must remember that our battles are not with flesh and blood. Paul reminds us in Ephesians:

"For we are not fighting against flesh-and-blood enemies, but against evil rulers and authorities of the unseen world, against mighty powers in this dark world, and against evil spirits in the heavenly places." Ephesians 6:12 (NLT)

To make jokes from a pulpit such as *'God created Adam and Eve, not Adam and Steve'* actually taunts, torments and shames the very person God is trying so hard to reach with his love, mercy, and tenderness. Christians are to always walk in love and kindness. God confirms in His word that His kindness is what leads to repentance.

Don't you see how wonderfully kind, tolerant, and patient God is with you? Does this mean nothing to you? Can't you see that his kindness is intended to turn you from your sin? Romans 2:4 (NLT)

We must realize, there is someone very precious to God, sitting in every single church in America trying to cope with these LGBTQ issues within themselves or their family. Many are breaking under the pressure. So many Christians are afraid or embarrassed to say anything and countless numbers are leaving churches altogether because they don't know what to do.

Because of the vast importance of this, I want to take a moment and encourage you today. If that's you or your family don't be afraid. God sees you. He loves you. He loves your family. He loves your loved one (or maybe it's you) that is struggling. Keep standing. Don't shrink back from God's word. Press into His promises. Every promise is yes and amen. Declare God's word over yourself and your loved ones. If you stay in love and don't compromise God's truth, you'll get the end result and you and/or your loved one will get freedom from that confusion.

God is faithful to His word. So declare, declare, declare the promises of God. Name yourself and your family in them. Find a good pastor or Bible believing friend that you can confide in, who will be a prayer partner with you. You are not alone. Be encouraged. Many are facing the same pressures, trials, and challenges. God will never let you down. Take heart, He'll meet you right where you and your family are.

Knowing this, it is essential every Christian willfully honor the covenant of God's plan for marriage in the voting booth. It may be helpful to remember that honoring God's definition of Biblical marriage between a man and woman doesn't mean you are betraying or being unkind to the one struggling with LGBTQ confusion or living that lifestyle. Be reassured, the most loving thing you can do is walk in truth, love, pray and vote God's will. God needs you to lovingly stand firm in that person's life, or your own life. Psalm 119: 130 (Complete Jewish Bible) says Gods words are a doorway that lets in light. The light of the word of God promises to deliver. It's the truth of the word we know that makes us free. You need to be immersed in God's truth and light for yourself and those around you.

I realize that the Supreme Court legalized same-sex marriage in the United States. But, Heaven's Court system did not and never will. Heaven's court system is not a democracy. Therefore, regardless of the earthly laws that have already been passed, make sure the candidate running for office believes and abides in the Bible's definition of marriage.

FINAL THOUGHTS

To Honor God in Every Election, Follow These Five Easy Steps

1. Pray for the leaders.
2. Register to vote and actively vote in all elections.
3. Vote for the candidate that will protect innocent life.
4. Vote for the candidate that will protect Israel.
5. Vote for the candidate that will honor the sanctity of Biblical marriage.

If Christians can accomplish this, all the other areas of concern will fall into place.

"But first and most importantly seek, aim at, strive after, His kingdom and His righteousness, His way of doing and being right—the attitude and character of God, and all these things will be given to you also." Matthew 6:32-33 (AMP)

Even if you do all these things and an election doesn't turn out the way you hoped. Just remember, that because you honored God by regularly praying for the leaders and casting your vote, you will be blessed for it. There will be a ripple effect of blessing for your family as well.

PRAYER FOR OUR NATION
Where there is unity, the Lord commands the blessing.
Psalm 133

It is so important to be in one accord for this nation. There is tremendous power available when God's children come into agreement and pray. Below is a prayer for America. Let's humble ourselves, lift our eyes to the Lord and pray in harmony over this land God has given us. I invite you to pray this prayer. God promises that when we gather together and agree down here on earth, concerning anything we ask for, that the Father in heaven will do it for us.

Sign the prayer in agreement at www.LizLemeryJoy.com/Sign-The-Prayer.

Almighty God,

We thank you for the privilege of living in the United States of America. You have blessed us with great prosperity, privilege, and influence among the nations. You have taken us through war and hardship and delivered us again and again. As Christians you have called us to be salt and light to the world.

We come to you now, knowing that we need your forgiveness. Your word says:

"If My people who are called by My name will humble themselves, and pray and seek My face, and turn from their wicked ways, then I will hear from heaven, and will forgive their sin and heal their land." 2 Chronicles 7:14

Our nation needs your healing restoration. We humble ourselves and repent of our lack of prayer. We ask you to forgive us for our complacency when it comes to voting. We turn away from every form of wickedness in our hearts, our thoughts, and our deeds. Forgive our sin God. Heal our land of every form of division and destruction.

Today, empower each one that signs this petition with your purity and power. We commit to stand up and vote the Bible. We will take our stand for righteousness that You Lord would be honored in our nation.

Revive us again LORD. Make our nation a beacon of hope and a light to all the nations. Let your destiny for the United States of America be fulfilled as we take our stand for freedom, liberty, and justice for all.

[1]We worship you, LORD. You are the God of Abraham, Isaac, and Jacob. In the name of Jesus, we pray,

Amen.

---

1 Prayer contributed by Sue Detweiler

ACKNOWLEDGEMENTS

To my husband Rob, I appreciate you and love you so much. Thank you for always helping me to thrive. You're my hero.

To my parents, John and Joan, thank you for always being wonderful, loving parents.

To Sandy Ross, my spiritual mother, mentor and friend, for your constant love and guidance.

To Kenneth Copeland Ministries, for sharing my interview on the BVOV broadcast, in the BVOV Magazine, and the Tim Show during the Washington DC Victory Campaign.

To Dr. Mark Jones, for your business acumen and guidance while preparing this book.

To George Amedore, my dear friend, for allowing me to speak during your campaign, resulting in a vision for this project.

To Joelle Amedore, also my very dear friend, for your faithful prayers, long talks, trips and laughter.

To Keith and Ruthanna Legg, for opening your pulpit repeatedly so I could share this message.

To Pastor Paul and Carolyn Tebbano, my pastors- for never compromising the truth of God's word. Harvest Church is a beacon of Light in Upstate New York.

To Sue Detweiler, my publisher and friend, for your willingness to take on this project. Thank you for leading me through this process and always ending phone calls with prayer.

To Rhonda Robinson, a wise woman with so much experience. I could listen to your wisdom for hours. Thank you for your kindness and patience.

To Britt Dodson, Thank you for your expertise, valuable input and graphics. I hope to work more with you in the future.

To Alyssa Avant, for your professionalism, website design and virtual assistance.

To my daughter Katie Joy and our friend Jason Cooper, for your keen eyes and help in choosing the idea for the cover, so it would catch the attention of young Christian voters.

ABOUT THE AUTHOR

Liz grew up in the gorgeous foothills of the Adirondack Mountains in Upstate New York. While attending college in Boston she met the love of her life, and now husband of 25 years. It was while her husband was an Active Duty Army physician that she began to fully appreciate the magnitude of freedoms we have in this great country called America. As they moved from military base to military base, Liz witnessed first-hand the sacrifices military men and women endured to maintain these freedoms on a daily basis. They selflessly gave and sacrificed with unparalleled patriotism for a land they proudly defended and protected.

Years later, while stationed at Ft. Sam Houston in Texas, she watched her home state be ruthlessly attacked by Islamic terrorists on TV. New York's Twin Towers decimated, the destruction of the Military's Headquarters at the Pentagon, and the heroic death of her friend's brave son on Flight 93. Countless lives taken as an act of war.

Since that time Liz has actively spoken and written about the importance of faith and freedom. She hosted youth groups and women's Bible studies in her home for years. She has been the guest on numerous radio shows, appeared on TBN in New York City and given sermons in churches on voting biblically. She has written a blog on

The Times Union on-line newspaper in the Capitol Region of New York, since 2009.

She created a "Vote the Bible" initiative while closely working with a Christian New York State Senate candidate, initiating communications with over 500 different churches, in order to encourage pastors, ministers, and Christians to take a Biblical stand at the voting booth.

Liz and her husband Rob currently reside in New York, where they actively support Christian outreach programs in their city. They are also involved in many charity causes promoting health and wellness in their community. Aside from writing and speaking, she enjoys spending time with her husband and four children, day hikes in the Adirondacks and dark French Roast coffee via her favorite French-press.

ADDENDUM

Democratic Party Platform 2016:

"https://www.demconvention.com/wp-content/uploads/2016/07/Democratic-Party-Platform-7.21.16-no-lines.pdf"https://www.demconvention.com/wp-content/uploads/2016/07/Democratic-Party-P...

Republican Party Platform 2016: "https ://prod-static-ngop-pbl.s3.amazonaws.com/media/documents/DRAFT_12_FINAL%5B1%5D-ben_1468872234.pdf"https://prod-static-ngop-pbl.s3.amazonaws.com/media/documents/DRAFT_12_FINA...

CPSIA information can be obtained
at www.ICGtesting.com
Printed in the USA
LVHW040138091020
668359LV00015B/982